SUGGESTIONS FOR GR

1. **THE ROOM** Discourage people from sittin[g] circle – all need to be equally involved.

2. **HOSPITALITY** Tea or coffee on arrival can be helpful at the first meeting. Perhaps at the end too, to encourage people to talk informally. Some groups might be more ambitious, taking it in turns to bring a dessert to start the evening with coffee at the end.

3. **THE START** If group members don't know each other well, some kind of 'icebreaker' might be helpful. For example, you might invite people to share something quite secular (where they grew up, holidays, hobbies, etc.). Place a time limit on this exercise.

4. **PREPARING THE GROUP** Take the group into your confidence, e.g. 'I've never done this before', or 'I've led lots of groups and each one has contained surprises'. Sharing vulnerability is designed to encourage all members to see the success of the group as their responsibility. Ask those who know that they talk easily to ration their contributions, and encourage the reticent to speak at least once or twice – however briefly. Explain that there are no 'right' answers and that among friends it is fine to say things that you are not sure about – to express half-formed ideas. However, if individuals choose to say nothing, that's all right too.

5. **THE MATERIAL** Encourage members to read each session *before* the meeting. It helps enormously if each group member has their own personal copy of this booklet (so the price is reduced either when multiple copies are ordered or if you order online). *There is no need to consider all the questions.* A lively exchange of views is what matters, so be selective. You can always spread a session over two or more meetings if you run out of time!

   For some questions you might start with a few minutes' silence to make jottings. Or you might ask members to talk in sub-groups of two or three, before sharing with the whole group.

6. **PREPARATION** Decide beforehand whether to distribute (or ask people to bring) paper, pencils, hymn books, etc. If possible, ask people in advance to read a Bible passage or lead in prayer, so that they can prepare.

7. **TIMING** Try to start on time and make sure you stick fairly closely to your stated finishing time.

8. **USING THE CD** The track markers on the CD (shown in the transcript booklet) will help you find your way around the CD very easily. For each of the sessions we recommend reading through the session in the booklet, before listening together to all of the relevant session on the CD. And then tackle the Questions for Groups.

YORK COURSES
Expecting Christ
A course in four sessions
written by Bishop David Wilbourne

Introduction

The writer Graham Greene famously said that there is always one moment in childhood where a door opens and lets the future in. In this course we look at several moments in our faith and lives where a door opens and lets Christ in, catching the sense of expectancy which not only comes at the season of Advent, but throughout the year. In particular, we will be thinking about how Christ can surprise us and meet us in four distinct contexts: in family, in ourselves, in prayer and in the end.

Some of the course gives clues about right places and wrong places where we might find Christ. But a substantial part of the course isn't so much to do with looking, but more about stilling ourselves and life's incessant clamour, so that we can be alert and open to Christ surprising us. It was only by night, when the busy world was hushed on that Judaean hillside, that the shepherds were able to hear the angels' song, directing them to find the one who was King of kings, yet born in a lowly stable.

Towards the end of his life, R S Thomas was vicar of Aberdaron at the very end of the Llyn peninsula, where West Wales juts out like a finger into the Irish Sea. This poet and priest, who must have had so many calls on his time, nevertheless used to sit for hours each spring at the very end of his patch, simply waiting to catch the first sight of migrating birds returning. My prayer is that this course will give you both the nerve to wait for Christ and also a sense of expectancy as to where you might find him – and be thrilled by what you find.

> *Come, thou long-expected Jesus,*
> *born to set thy people free.*
> *From our fears and sins release us,*
> *let us find our rest in thee.*
>
> *(Charles Wesley 1707-1788)*

SESSION 1

Expecting Christ in family

The challenge of scripture

I'm sure there was a *Reader's Digest* book called *The Best Bits of the Bible*, which gave me the idea for another tome: *Bits of the Bible Which Make Your Toes Curl!*

For instance, what about that familiar family story – God ordering Abraham to sacrifice his beloved only son Isaac (Genesis 22.1–19). I find it pretty hard to take. 'If God told me to do that to my child, I'd tell him to get lost!' a gruff Teessider once exclaimed to me.

OK, you can see the incident as a turning point in the history of religion, with Abraham moving on from a pagan primitive bloodlust faith in a god who delights in child-sacrifice to a faith in a loving Yahweh, the God who cradles the world in his tender embrace. But even then, the episode still leaves a nasty taste in my mouth. There's a dark side to the story which remains, despite my liberal interpretation.

At Sinai, only one biblical book later, God thunders: 'Thou shalt not murder.' Yet here we have him inciting Abraham to murder to test his loyalty. I'm sorry, but this incident doesn't paint God in a very moral light, and I want to argue that God is actually more moral than this. And so is humankind, a humankind which I hope is not so easily duped to commit infanticide.

And then there's all that stuff in 1 Samuel where poor old King Saul just can't get it right (1 Samuel 15). Ordered by God to kill every Amalekite man, woman, child and beast, he spares some of them, and is punished by having the kingship ultimately taken away from him. Had Saul done what God ordered him to do, we'd have indicted him for war crimes. Because he proved too merciful, God shunned him.

Yes, it's a complicated story, and Saul might have had some murky ulterior motives: sparing the best beasts and best humans to take as booty, maybe even to sacrifice to his God made in Samuel's tetchy image. But even so, God doesn't come across in this incident in a good light; and I would want to say the God I know is much more merciful and life-affirming than this.

The challenge of strong words

Some wag once claimed that one sure thing happens as you turn the pages of the Old Testament – God mellows with age. Whatever … but by the time you reach the New Testament you expect God to behave himself. And yet we have Jesus surprising us in Luke's Gospel. Luke's Gospel has been described as the Gospel of the *Anawim* (the Gospel of the humble ones). Little people loom large with Luke. Luke has a longer cast list of little people than that of *The Lord of the Rings*: barren Elizabeth and

Zechariah; a virgin called Mary; shepherds who were beyond the religious pale watching their flocks by day and by night, failing to observe the Sabbath, getting themselves unclean by wandering into Gentile territory to rescue their lost sheep; Simeon and Anna, old and dotty and ignored; women of the streets; prodigal sons; detested Samaritans; terrorists who were getting their just deserts, gasping with their last breath, 'Jesus, remember me when you come into your kingdom'. A whole family of little people, forgotten ones, who are not forgotten by Christ.

A famous commentator on Luke's Gospel describes it as 'the Gospel of pardons': the big tent Gospel, which even goes so far as to show mercy to the cruellest enemies, with Luke the only Gospel to feature Jesus' words from the cross: 'Father forgive them, for they know not what they do.'

But in this gentlest of gentle Gospels I am brought up short by the following words:

'Whoever comes to me
and does not hate father and mother,
wife and children,
brothers and sisters,
yes, and even life itself,
cannot be my disciple.'   (Luke 14.26)

Jesus doesn't say:

'Unless you neglect father and
    mother,
unless you keep in perspective wife
    and children,
unless you limit your loyalty to
    brothers and sisters
unless you are realistic about your
    life/work balance ...'

He says *'hate'*, with all the vehemence connected with the word. He pulls no punches whatsoever. Oh dear, what on earth do you do with that text?

First, I have to be honest and say, 'I can't go with you there, Lord. We have to part company at this point. No doubt you had your reasons, but I can't go along with you.'

I sense it is better to be honest rather than taking the words to mean the opposite of what they actually mean. You know the sort of thing: when Jesus said that it was easier for a camel to go through the eye of a needle than for a rich man to inherit the kingdom of heaven, he didn't really mean the actual eye of a needle. He meant that low archway into Jerusalem called the Eye of a Needle: so narrow, so low, that a camel had to be relieved of some of its load before it could get through. Jesus wasn't condemning riches *per se*, just saying you can't take it all with you.

It's a very seductive argument that tones down the harshness of Jesus' bald saying. But there's one tiny flaw. In the history of Jerusalem there has never been an archway called the Eye of a Needle!

Second, I also believe it is better to be honest than to pretend – to bluff. Peter proclaimed, 'Lord, even if I have to die with you, I will never deny you.' But he couldn't deliver that promise. He went back on his brave words and did deny him.

I feel that it is better to be honest to God, be realistic and know our limitations, rather than to lie. God's call for us all is only discovered when we stop playing games, when we stop pretending and are honest with ourselves, and so with God.

Third, odd though Jesus' words about neglecting father, mother and the rest of the family are, I can imagine a scenario where they cropped up. Everybody proffering their excuses: 'Well, I'd like to go along with you, Jesus, but I'm too busy, I've got friends coming round to dinner, I've got to pick up the children from school, it's our anniversary, I need to clean out my parents' home.'

And faced with a thousand and one domestic excuses, and seeing the dawning kingdom slip away from him because of his followers' apathy, I can imagine him snapping, 'Look here, unless you hate …'

When people say to me, 'I can't come to church on Sunday, I've got to cook the dinner for our guests', I have to say I'm sorely tempted to speak as Jesus spoke: 'Unless you hate your guests …'

Fourth, if we're honest, as I think we should be, we have to admit that our loyalties, even within the family, have to be divided.

The challenge of being in a family

The decisions we face are never quite as extreme as in the film *Sophie's Choice*, where the cruel Gestapo force the Jewess Sophie to decide which of her two children is to be condemned to the gas chamber. She has to let one child go, so that she and her remaining child can live. She effectively trades one child for life.

That's an extreme example, but families do trade. 'Shall we look after Grandad at home or admit him to a nursing home?' There's no easy solution to that one. Whichever way you jump involves someone's sacrifice. My family moved in the middle of my A-levels. My dad wanted a parish where he was in sole charge. I sympathised with his desire, but I found it a very tough transition from one sixth form to another.

What I'm saying is that however well motivated we may feel, sometimes our family and friends get hurt because of our pursuit of the greater good. We never set out to hate them, but sometimes the situation can make people feel as if they were hated. 'Nobody wants me, nobody loves me,' cries Grandad in his old people's home.

Finally, I would like to have the audacity to come back at Jesus, with a sort of prayer-with-attitude: 'I can understand, Lord, how you feel your kingdom is losing out because of all our domestic ties. But far from being a distraction from your kingdom of love, I see my family as an outpost of that kingdom, schooling me in its qualities. Loving, rather than hating mother, father, wife, children, brothers and sisters – and even myself – makes me blossom as your child.'

Only by loving do we enter into true humanity, and only by entering true humanity can we share Christ's divinity.

As an immature 26-year-old I asked Rachel to marry me; Rachel, whom I'd met at a Lent course where we'd been addressed by the most tedious bishop in Christendom. My chat-up line, though original, has come back to haunt me: 'Wasn't that bishop boring!'

But one of the reasons I asked her to marry me was that I felt very very strongly that marriage, and the family that went with it, would give me the best shot I would ever have in this life of receiving and giving the love championed by St Paul in 1 Corinthians 13 – a love which is patient, kind, not self-seeking, which keeps no score of wrongs, but delights in the truth.

People misquote St Augustine's famous saying: 'Love and do what you will.' They think that it should be: 'Love God and do what you will'. But if you love with the sort of love that 1 Corinthians 13 champions, then the word 'God' is really superfluous, because that sort of love is already divine.

The challenge of the kingdom of God

In my book, the kingdom of God won't dawn despite family and friends, but because of them and through them, as fellow citizens of God's country.

In a play about the life of the seventeenth-century Welsh mystic, Morgan Lloyd, the playwright charts his hero's progress through the religious controversies of that age. Not surprisingly, by the end of the play Lloyd has reached a state of total disillusionment and despair. He pours out his agony in a desperate plea to God: 'O God, come, come, bring your holy death to kiss me to your own clear, shining light.'

There is complete silence, and then Lloyd's little son comes on to the stage. He calls to his father quietly and affectionately and Lloyd looks at him, as though hearing his voice for the first time. He stretches out his hand to the boy, who takes it. Then his small daughter comes in and calls to him, and he offers her his other hand. Morgan's wife joins them, carrying their baby. She gives the child to her husband. Cradling the little one in his arms, he begins to sing her a nursery rhyme. The others join in.

The playwright, John Gwilym Jones, tells us that the play should end on 'a note of quiet, affectionate joy'. The playwright's message is that God will not be found in abstruse and bitter theological and political wrangling. He may, however, be found in the loving kindness that is present in close human relationships at their best.

When his son calls him, Lloyd recognises the voice of love which is the voice of God. He sees that the things which he had thought significant, the agonising soul-searching and the anguished spiritual quest with all its complex doctrinal confrontations, were really irrelevant. God was not present in them, but was present in the little family whom Lloyd had neglected and ignored for so long.

'Unless you hate father and mother,
    wife and children,
brothers and sisters you cannot be
    my disciple.'

As Jesus howls those understandable words, it is other howls that I hear and am moved by. The howls of a new-born baby in a peasant's stable in Bethlehem, the howls of a man being cruelly crucified at Calvary as his anguished mother looks on. Those howls at both ends of life's spectrum break my heart and move me to be tender to the Christ who dwells in all God's children, and through whom his kingdom will one day dawn.

At their ordination in the Anglican Church, priests and deacons, as representatives of the whole people of God, are asked: 'Will you strive to fashion your own life and that of your household according to the way of Christ?'

I've never gone for that question in a big way, since I think vicarage families have enough to put up with without Revd Dad or Revd Mum fashioning them. Unless you've been a 'vicarage kid' you may not know about the abuse they take at school, the abuse they sometimes have to take from the congregation who expect them to be holier than them.

When my father was first ordained, he served in East Hull. I was six. On my first day at my new school the children all ganged up around me: 'Na, na, your dad's a vicar.' 'He isn't a vicar,' I replied in all seriousness,

'He's just been ordained a deacon and is the assistant curate of Marfleet.' The earnestness of my reply and the complexities of Anglicanism floored them. They went away, the oldest first, and I never had any trouble with them after that.

But don't tell me about clergy fashioning their families. That road is scattered with too many victims. If I were allowed to rewrite the ordination service I would instead ask, 'Will you allow Christ to fashion you through those around you? Will you be as Christ to those you love, and see none other than Christ in those who love you?'

Such a vow is far far bigger than ordination. It challenges us all as we strive to be fashioned by family and friends. One former Dean of Durham quipped: 'When Jesus told us to love our enemies, he was good enough to give us relatives to practise on!' But on a more serious note, a good and brief self-examination at the end of every day is to ask: 'What of Christ have I seen in those around me this day? And what of Christ have those around me seen in me?'

Expecting Christ in family and friends will be the making or breaking of us.

Anoint and cheer our soiled face
With the abundance of thy grace:
Keep far our foes, give peace at home;
Where thou art guide no ill can come.

(John Cosin 1594-1672, based on *Veni Creator Spiritus*)

QUESTIONS FOR GROUPS

Now that you've read this session, we recommend you listen together to Session 1 on the course CD all the way through, before tackling the Questions for Groups below. Some groups will address all the questions. That's fine. Others prefer to select just a few and spend longer on each. That's fine, too. Horses for (York) Courses!

BIBLE READING: 1 Corinthians 13.4-12

1. Do Christians actually need the Old Testament? If we do, how should we understand and use it – as history, as allegory, as literal truth, as poetry, for its beauty, or what?

2. **Read Luke 14.26.** David says he can't go along with Jesus' demand to hate his family [CD track 5 & p. 4]. Does he have to? Or is Jesus making a different – though related – point in an attention-grabbing way? In any case, is it an option for a Christian to reject parts of the Gospel story?

3. If you came from a Christian family, has it been an advantage? If you didn't, has it been a disadvantage [tracks 7 and 8 on the CD]?

4. Have you ever found yourself in a dilemma where you have found it impossible to satisfy everyone? If so, how did you resolve it? Are you convinced by David's prayer-with-attitude? [p. 5]

5. 'Will you allow Christ to fashion you through those around you?' [track 10 and p. 7] Do you find this a helpful way of thinking about Christian formation and growth?

6. 'What of Christ can I see in others and what of Christ can others see in me?' How helpful, or otherwise, do you find this self-analysis? [track 14 and p. 7]

7. Do you expect to meet Christ, or see him reflected, in family? Can you share with the group any such occasion or situation?

8. Towards the end of this session David adds 'friends' to 'family'. Do you have the same expectations of your friends?

9. The suggested bible text at the top of the page is the famous *Hymn to love* in 1 Corinthians 13. Is it realistic to set this as a benchmark for how family relationships should be?

Expecting Christ

SESSION 2
Expecting Christ in me

Three surprising facts

Recently a local radio station featured me in their Desert Island Discs slot. Clearly austerity has begun to bite, because I was only allowed to choose two records instead of the proverbial eight! Instead of the remaining six records, I had to come up with three surprising facts about myself – really, *really* surprising.

It's a good game to play. Your first response is to think: 'There's nothing surprising about me!' Which is a bit of a sad verdict, that you can surprise no one, not even God.

My first surprising fact was that, taking my cue from that great father of the Church, Norman Tebbit, who said 'Get on your bike!', I thoroughly enjoy cycling.

Though Jesus' preferred mode of transport was a donkey, setting a precedent for humility, people expect bishops to turn up in posh cars. So they get a bit surprised when I roll up for a confirmation on my bicycle. Once I cycled to a service in heavy rain (Cardiff being Cardiff) cowering in my cagoule. As I was parking my bike in the church porch a churchwarden came up and ticked me off: 'You can't park your cycle there, we've got the bishop coming!'

But I absolutely love cycling. I came to it late in life, so I have all the enthusiasm of a late-in-the day convert. Not only do I relish the exercise, but also the ability to go anywhere under my own steam, getting there far more quickly than walking.

There used to be an advertising slogan, 'Get away from it all on the train', but I get away from it all on the bike: no computers, no phones, no insurmountable problems pestering me. Cycling allows me to 'be' before God.

I'm not prescribing cycling as a spiritual exercise for everyone: different strokes for different folks. But I guess for many of us there is a particular something which will give us that necessary space amidst the clamour and hyperactivity of over-busy lives. Maybe carving out such space is a rehearsal for periods of life when, because of age or illness or grief, we simply can't be busy. Although having inactivity thrust upon us can be immensely frustrating, suddenly having time on our hands need not be lost time, but found time, as we discover, to use William Vanstone's phrase, 'the stature of waiting'. The letter to the Hebrews talks about every Sabbath being a preparation for the ultimate Sabbath, eternal rest (Hebrews 4.1–11).

My second surprising fact is that I absolutely adore 'doing the Math', as they say in America.

Again, Maths was something I never expected to enjoy. My mum's education had been interrupted by frequent bombing raids in the war and so she had never really got to grips with Maths. Until the day she died she had a terror of decimals, a fear she tried to pass on to me as an infant: 'Never mind about long division, you just wait until those decimals come along!' They sounded worse than the Daleks!

But I found them a friend rather than a foe, chiefly because we had a Maths teacher who was more than a bit of a comedian and replaced the terror that most children have of Maths with laughter. With the result that I find Maths irresistible, often tricky, but an activity I just love. When I'm doing Maths I get the sense that for this I was made, so much so that I've always fancied teaching Maths. Maybe I'm naive, and had I taken it up as a career would soon have become disillusioned!

But doing Maths in my head has certainly kept me alive during many a tedious church meeting, where you sit there sympathising with Jesus in the tomb, longing for resurrection. Maths stops me dying of boredom!

But tricky though Maths is, the solutions to some of even the most complex problems are so often stunningly simple to the extent that if the ultimate solution is complicated, it's probably wrong. After all, $E=mc^2$, which is the closest Einstein got to the secret of the universe, contains just three letters and one number.

They say that to do Maths is to enter into the mind of God, which makes me wonder whether we make faith – the Christian faith and all faiths – too complicated, too off-putting, and whether the heart of faith is really quite simple. Interestingly, both Cardinal Basil Hume and a former Archbishop of York, John Habgood, towards the end of their ministry, extolled saying the Lord's Prayer as both the heart and the goal of their spirituality. Barely seventy words that said it all, better than a thousand sermons or books.

If you had to state your faith in a single sentence, what would that be? I once asked a vicar that, prior to a confirmation: 'How would you sum up all your confirmation classes in one sentence?' 'Behave yourselves,' she replied with a great grin.

'God loves you,' would be my three words. The disciples of John the letter-writer gathered around his deathbed, wanting him to give them a final word. 'God is love,' he gasped. 'But you've said that already,' they complained. 'There is nothing more to be said,' he replied.

My final surprising fact is that I like mending things. Last year's big achievement was mending the washing machine at our cottage in Wensleydale. The machine came to a grinding halt mid-cycle and no amount of cajoling, turning on and off, hitting with mallets, etc. would persuade it to resume.

I slid the machine into the middle of our tiny kitchen and proceeded to take it apart while the rest of the family were trying to consume their Sunday supper, shielding their tomato soup from nuts, bolts, wires and other sundry projectiles.

The contacts on the on/off switch had burnt out, so I re-routed the wiring through the rinse-hold switch, with the result that the latter switch now turns the machine on and off. What was formerly the on/off switch now acts as the rinse-hold feature, but only if you want to hold the rinse for an eternity!

I like taking things apart when they have gone wrong – and often manage to put them back together again, although any repair is definitely in the Heath Robinson category! It's a journey of discovery; often I marvel at the design, the ingenuity of the person who put it together in the first place. Invariably I am faced with an array of nuts and bolts and screws and wonder how I am ever going to get the thing back together again. Yet strangely I am never afraid, because whenever I am mending things, I feel that this is where I am meant to be, for this I was born.

I suppose it's a bit akin to enjoying Maths, believing in your heart of hearts that you are going to work through to a solution. Whether it's driven by my resurrection faith, or whether my resurrection faith derives from that, who knows. I suppose in Christ all things are mendable, all things are resurrectable.

If God could pull the ultimate Easter Day comeback with the mangled body of Jesus, then he can fix anything. Even ourselves: we are all too prone to be hard on ourselves, beat ourselves up, think of ourselves as beyond the pale when it comes to Christ. But however bad we may or may not be, the Christ who is within each of his children never gives up, calling and recalling us, reminding us of his desire that nothing, however broken, can be separated from his love. 'Everything is resurrectable' is the heart of all our faith.

Two enlightening records

And my two records? The first was *In Dreams* by Roy Orbison. Although he died over a quarter of a century ago, he is a legend, because of his unique voice which effortlessly spans several octaves and because lament is his trademark. He is usually singing about loss, putting into haunting song tragedy acted out in his own personal life.

As a society I think we have lost the ability to lament, to catch the tragic in song – not to wave a magic wand and make it all right, but simply to record the poignant and the lost, giving prominence and significance to what seems futile and senseless.

And, often, daring to lament is the first halting step towards restoration: Jairus in the Gospels, lamenting his dying daughter (Luke 8.41-42 & 49-56); the centurion lamenting his dying favourite servant (Matthew 8.5-13); the woman lamenting that she had been bleeding for twelve long years, daring just to touch the hem of Jesus' cloak (Luke 8.43-48); the father of the epileptic son, lamenting his plaintive plea, 'Lord, I have faith. Help me where faith falls short' (Matthew 17.14-18). It is at the very point when these people voice the utter futility of their situation that healing dawns.

The Psalms were a masterclass at lament, with their 'My God, my God, why have you forsaken me?' (Psalm 22.1.) Legend has it that most were written by my namesake, King David. I am sure if we had a recording of him from three millennia back, he would sound exactly like Roy Orbison! *In Dreams* is such a lament, dreaming of a lost love never to be recovered. But in that particular song, terrific hope is tinged with loss.

Dreaming is a very Christian activity: dreaming of a world where God will reign, where his kingdom will come, where there will be no more tears, no more sorrow, no more war, no more poverty. Some dreams! And yet undoubtedly they are the dreams of which God is made, and dreaming the dreams of God is a sort of prayer, a real sort of prayer. Maybe 'Lord, let me make your dreams come true this day,' is the very best sort of prayer.

My other record couldn't be further from Roy. It's virtually the European National Anthem these days. In the 1970s when I first encountered *Ode to Joy* from Beethoven's Choral Symphony it was less well known. As a teenager I was very taken with it, not least because our German teacher had told us how he had got Grade 1 French O-level by learning the list of ingredients on the French side of the HP sauce bottle. A question had come up about a meal in his French oral exam and he was off, rattling off a somewhat acerbic but obviously convincing menu.

HP sauce didn't run to German ingredients, so I learnt *Ode to Joy* instead, and hoped against hope that 'joy' would come up in my German oral, and off I would run. I could even sing it, *'Freude schöne Gotterfunken, Tochter aus Elysium …'*.

Alas, the examiner asked me about the Ruhr, the distinctly joyless industrial region in Germany and, politician though I am, even I couldn't bring *Freude schöne Gotterfunken* (*beautiful spark of the gods*) into my answer.

But joy has stayed with me, because it is both our desire and our call as Christians to be joyful because we are Christ's; the Christ who loves us so much he can't take his eyes off us. It is not a sugary joy, turning a blind eye to all of life's tragedies, pretending that all is lovely in the garden when all is clearly not. It is simply a joy which comes of being Christ's, which kicks everything else into touch.

One Christ for all

Luke 9 and Hebrews 12 boldly state that when Christ set his face toward Jerusalem and toward the ultimate suffering of the cross, it was for the joy set before him – joy because this was God's purpose for him and the world, that he was the lead actor, the only actor in God's ultimate rescue. Go for joy!

Bad things happen, good things happen, that's life. How we respond is up to us. So many people have received so many knocks in life, bruises upon their bruises, yet still have a quiet, a definite joy. So many people are blessed so richly, and yet are utterly miserable.

I remember my dad in his first parish running a garden party in 1966. The sun shone, all records were broken, no one died fighting over the cream teas. Happily exhausted at the end of it all, my Dad faced a miserable old man who pointed an accusing finger at him: 'This is all very well, but what would you have done if it had rained?!'

There's always one, an out-of-work U-Boat commander looking for a war. In my last parish we had so much going for us, which one or two ecclesiastical terrorists repeatedly tried to hijack. At one stage I decided to go on the offensive, and at our garden party have a-most-miserable-person-in-the-parish competition. True to form, the most miserable person in the parish complained about having a-most-miserable-person-in-the-parish competition, nicely proving my point! But by going for Christ's joy, lock, stock and barrel, we render ourselves ineligible for such a competition.

Expecting Christ in me may seem idiosyncratic, if not blasphemous. I have worked with clergy who resolutely avoid the personal, from not mentioning even the name of the deceased at a funeral, down to never using personal pronouns in their sermons. 'People want to see Jesus, not me,' they claim. And they have a fair point – preachers perpetually in entertainment mode, desperately seeking the approval of their audience, can eclipse Christ and his Gospel.

And yet the heart of that Gospel is that God is personal, the Holy Spirit has a local accent, speaking and acting through you and me. Expecting Christ in me is about recovering our nerve to seek Christ within each and every one of us, and to be surprised by all the bicycles and Maths and mending stuff and Roy Orbisons and Ninth Symphonies, up there with the stables and shepherds and fishermen and carpenters' shops and crosses and garden tombs which reveal him in all his fullness.

QUESTIONS FOR GROUPS
BIBLE READINGS: Romans 8.9-11 and Galatians 2.19-20

1. Do you ever feel the need to be alone? Where do you go to be alone?

2. Do you ever have a sense of God being there? And anyway, where is 'there'? Do you mean there as in 'up there/existing' or there as in 'with you/alongside you'?

3. How would you sum up your faith in one short sentence? What's at the heart of it? And if you don't have a faith – or aren't sure of it – what/how would you like it to be?

4. What do you make of the biscuit-barrel story on the CD [track 19]?

5. With the Enniskillen reference in mind [track 21], have you ever been part of a collective spiritual experience? Or do you know anyone who has?

6. David doesn't seem to mind taking risks – for instance with repairing his washing machine. Are you a risk-taker and, if so, in what areas?

7. Is everything resurrectable? What about really bad things such as war crimes, violence, abuse, terrorism – are these things and the people who commit them resurrectable? Or are there some things or people too dead for God to resurrect?

8. Do you believe in heaven? If so, what will it be like?

9. *'It is at the very point when these people voice the utter futility of their situation that healing dawns.'* [p. 11]. Is this your experience? Can you share a time when futility turned into hope?

10. *'Dreaming is a very Christian activity.'* Is David actually talking about daydreaming? Or are we to trust real dreams which come when we are asleep?

11. How could you 'go for Christ's joy' today? What would it mean in terms of home life, work, family, church?

12. Can you see Christ in other people? Do you think they can see Christ in you? What does he look like?

13. Is Christ personal? And what does that mean to you [track 30]?

SESSION 3
Expecting Christ in prayer

Hopeless at prayer

'Things ain't what they used to be!' We're all prone to wallow in nostalgia. I heard of a priest who thought himself young but then found himself coming out with phrases such as: 'Well, in my day … , or 'Well, when I was trained, and trained properly, mind you', or, 'Well, when I was a curate …' I suppose I've reached that certain age, both in my life and in my ministry, when I too am tempted to pronounce on the past golden age which was my day. But all I can say with any certainty is this:

After 30 years' ministry, I am absolutely appalled … how hopeless I am at prayer!

There's really no excuse. If I were newly ordained, I could hope that I would improve, find more time for prayer once I got the hang of things, read edifying spiritual books, prioritise my life and pray. But after three decades of good intentions I realise that unless a sea change comes along things are not going to get much better. There's really no excuse, no excuse at all. 'Will you be diligent at prayer?' I was asked at my ordination. Tut, tut!

'Well, don't worry, you must be good at other things,' I hear people say. That doesn't comfort me at all, since just as a teacher's chief work is to teach, and a doctor's to heal, the chief work of a priest, minister, pastor is to pray, and I should be sacked because I am so bad at it.

'You're not that bad,' I hear others say. 'Hearing you pray is a spiritual experience.' People tend to say things like that to bishops! But even if it's true it's nothing to do with me, more to do with God taking my impoverished words and thoughts and breathing life into them, a divine lone ranger riding in to sort out the mess that Wilbourne has made.

'Oh come on,' someone else will say, 'There must have been high points of prayer in three decades of ministry. Don't be so hard on yourself, focus on them.'

First of all, I would want to go far further back than my ordination, since prayer is not just for clergy but for everyone. In theory 'religious professionals' are released from other things to concentrate on prayer, but it is not a solo activity. Their praying should be contagious, drawing others into prayer.

And if I'm honest there have been odd moments, glorious moments. When I was just eleven I watched the mass funeral of those poor Welsh children, 116 of them, suffocated when a huge pile of mining debris slid down the mountainside above the village of Aberfan, virtually demolishing the Pantglas Junior School. My little boy's heart went out to them. The mourners sang the hymn *Jesu, lover of my soul*, then unfamiliar to me, but I was so taken with the haunting tune that I tracked it down in my father's *English Hymnal* and played and played and played it on my recorder – I must have driven my parents mad! But I guess through the hymn I felt in some inchoate, unspoken way that God was there in that pain, and that in some mysterious way I was allied with, caught by, the sorrowing heart of God. This is prayer as tuning in, empathising with God's woundedness: I often return to that, or would do more often if only I had more time … .

Perseverance in prayer

Then another memory from childhood: watching my father, a Church of England vicar, say his prayers, morning by morning, evening by evening. I always thought my father was bound to be made Archbishop of Canterbury for such holiness but he never was. But that didn't seem to worry him.

Even in the grottiest and most forlorn parishes, day after day he prayed. Sometimes I said Morning Prayer with him, just to keep him company. On those occasions I felt very proud, sharing in this important business of prayer.

Christopher C is a jolly good sort
and revels in every conceivable sport.
He governs a school with the highest of aims
to teach English boys to be manly at games.
And feels when his finer emotions are warm,
that he might get ordained as a matter
  of form.

Jeremy J is a diligent priest
with a pastoral heart full of love for the least.
He comforts the anxious and succours
  the sick,
he buries the dead and he visits the quick,
for year after year in his parish he stays
and he prays and he prays and he prays and
  he prays.

Christopher C like a gentleman true
has married the niece of the Bishop of Q,
is whirled in a flash to a prominent perch
and given the charge of a priory church,
although it must always be carefully shown
that he achieved this honour by his
  merit alone.

Jeremy J is a diligent priest
with a pastoral heart full of love for the least.
He comforts the anxious and succours
  the sick,
he buries the dead and he visits the quick,
for year after year in his parish he stays
and he prays and he prays and he prays and
  he prays.

Christopher C we are proud to relate
has reached the archidiaconal state,
and hopes if he pulls the appropriate string
to gain the episcopal mitre and ring.
And who would begrudge to this
  gentleman true
the right to his honours where honour is due.

Jeremy J is a diligent priest
with a pastoral heart full of love for the least.
He comforts the anxious and succours
  the sick,
he buries the dead and he visits the quick,
for year after year in his parish he stays
and he prays and he prays and he prays and
  he prays …

(*Ecce Sacerdos Magnus* by S J Forest in *What's the Use?*, Mowbray 1955)

I found prayer very comforting at university. College is a big step for any young person – leaving home, fending for yourself, competing with academic excellence. It can be overwhelming for some. I remember praying and feeling a tremendous warmth and reassurance. And as the university years went by, people I knew, even those training for ministry, were very scathing about prayer. But I could never let go that prayer mattered – mattered supremely, in that the overwhelming evidence of mystics through the ages is that persevering in prayer is the very place where they catch the occasional glimpse of God.

RS Thomas, majestically as ever, portrays this feeling in the language of medieval chivalry. The pray-er is cast as a rather diffident knight whose quest is to rescue his beloved, a princess imprisoned in a high tower. He is diffident because he is unsure she is there at all.

Prayers like gravel
flung at the sky's
window, hoping to attract
the loved one's
attention. But without
visible plaits to let
down for the believer
to climb up,
to what purpose open
that far casement?
I would
have refrained long since
but that peering once
through my locked fingers
I thought that I detected
the movement of a curtain.

My experience of prayer in ministry is really a very poor show indeed. My daily prayers, my daily Bible reading so often seem perfunctory.

But from time to time I'll be reading some Bible text, finding the prayer for the day, and something will leap out at me, and judge me, or inspire me, or give me the stamina to start again. And those moments make me realise it's important to stick at it.

Discovering prayer

After ten years in ministry something disturbed my prayer life. Much to my surprise, in 1991 I was made chaplain to the then Archbishop of York, John Habgood. Being an archbishop's chaplain is an ecclesiastical cross between Bernard and Sir Humphrey of *Yes, Prime Minister* fame, or playing Lewis to the Archbishop's Morse.

The day began at Bishopthorpe Palace with prayer in the thirteenth-century chapel. There were usually just the three of us, the Archbishop, the Press Officer and me, taking turns to lead Morning Prayer, read the lessons, lead the intercessions. Having to pray before an archbishop brought me up short and drove me to find the words: drove me also to listen to his words, words which seemed to have been long pondered and found to have immense weight. I was driven too to listen to others' words – hymn writers, poets, novelists – whose words I used, learnt off by heart, when my words were scarce. There's a handful of hymns which are immense prayers.

I daren't count up how many retreats I had to organise, but after a couple of years as Archbishop's chaplain I decided to restrict my retreat nights away to twenty per year. Because I didn't sleep well I always used to get up early and steal into chapel and just drink from the dark God-filled silence and feel a tremendous quenching. A lot of retreats were to do with those who were training for ordination, and I used to watch those who breezed into chapel five minutes before Morning Prayer started, who then looked superior to those who tumbled in two minutes before Morning Prayer started. Some retreats involved the senior staff, bishops, archdeacons, deans, who also often breezed in just five minutes before! Such retreats brought home both my need for prayer and the fact that I wasn't the only one whose practice was impoverished.

We all ought to be sacked. That most prayerful of archbishops, Michael Ramsey, was asked how long he prayed every morning. 'Just, just, two minutes,' came the shocking answer. 'But, but, but, it takes me 45 minutes to get there.' I'm comforted that such a spiritual giant found the going hard.

Sometimes when I pray with people I feel as if I drink from their goodness.

Expecting Christ

Group prayer in my own tradition invariably happens in church buildings, serious houses on serious earth, focusing on Holy Communion. You might say we have too many Communions, and yet I find each celebration never fails to nourish me, to make God close as touch. For me every Communion, focusing on how God in Christ was wounded at Calvary, harks back to my Aberfan experience, allying God's woundedness with our own woundedness, aching for resurrection.

Surprised by prayer

I've mentioned before how my greatest aid to prayer is my bicycle. Cycling down some of the 1:3 slopes really does drive you to prayer! Actually the sheer thrill drives you to prayer. But when I get on my bike, then nothing else but God can get to me. I learnt to cycle late in life, and it surprised me with prayer.

That's the funny thing about prayer. I wonder sometimes whether it's something we do – 'Oh dearie me, I haven't done enough prayer' – or whether prayer actually finds us, seeks us out, like love. All those teenagers desperately looking for love, when actually it's love that finds you; all those Christians desperately looking for prayer, when actually it's prayer that finds you. Prayer seeks us out in the people we meet, the situations we encounter, the places we visit. We dread prayer as a duty, and then we're surprised by it discovering us as a joy. Prayer, not a duty, but a joy, finding us.

'They tell me, Lord, that when I seem
To be in speech with you,
Since but one voice is heard, it's all a dream,
One talker aping two.

Sometimes it is, yet not as they
Conceive it. Rather, I
Seek in myself the things I hoped to say,
But lo, my wells are dry.

Then seeing me empty, you forsake
The listener's role and through
My dumb lips breathe and into
*   utterance wake*
The thoughts I never knew.

And thus you neither need reply,
Nor can; thus, while we seem
Two talkers, thou art One forever, and I
no dreamer, but thy dream.'

This poem, quoted by C S Lewis in his *Letters to Malcolm: Chiefly on Prayer*, takes its cue from Romans 8.26: 'We do not know what we ought to pray, but the Spirit himself intercedes for us with groans that words cannot express.'

Found by prayer

Found by prayer, not a duty but a joy.

I'm not sure whether prayer can be forced. As I said, I found it an unforgettable comfort when I went to university, and it has been a comfort at other times of crisis. But not in all crises. In some crises I have prayed and actually felt more, rather than less, addled, as if prayer wasn't a relief or a distraction from trouble, but was actually drawing you more into the centre of the storm.

I often think about Jesus' prayer from the cross: 'My God, my God, why have you forsaken me?' and wonder whether that was that sort of prayer in which God wasn't out there riding to the rescue, but was actually impaled on the storm of terror with his son. Perhaps I shy away from prayer because such prayer frightens me. I fear prayer could land me in a lot more trouble.

St Luke's Gospel features a story which Jesus invented to encourage his disciples to stick at prayer: the parable of the unjust judge. Even the unjust judge gave in to the woman whose constant pleading was wearing him out (Luke 18.1-8). Stick at prayer.

However much a failure I feel, I have stuck at it for over 30 years' ministry, and I know that sticking at it will never leave me. I want to encourage you to stick at it too, because at the end of the day, the end of our day, prayer is all that matters.

At the end of the day, though, it is quite healthy to laugh at our shortcomings, to smile at the pathetic faith, even amongst his ordained ministers, that the Son of Man will find on our earth when he comes. As this story by Rabbi Lionel Blue marvellously illustrates:

New neighbours moved in next door to the Browns. Very holy neighbours, Orthodox Jews, who came with all the Jewish trimmings, including a box on their door-post.

'Is it for letters?' the Browns asked.

'Oh no,' Mr Cohen explained. 'That box is a Mezuzah, which has accompanied our every move of house, and contains our most holy texts. Every time we enter and leave our house, we open the box and read and pray them.'

'Can I have a look in?'' Mr Brown asks.

'Well, yes,' Mr Cohen agreed, hesitatingly.

Mr Brown opens the box, empty except for a tiny screwed-up paper, which he unscrews and reads out, with a puzzled look:

'Help, I'm a prisoner in a Mezuzah factory!'

On a more serious note, in Orthodox Judaism, during any act of worship, a man is set at the synagogue door, simply to wait and watch out for the Messiah. Before leading any act of worship, I love to stand outside the church door and watch. In many ways it's the most prayerful activity of my day, simply watching for Christ. Perhaps that's the essence of prayer, pausing and expecting none other than Christ to surprise us. To give R S Thomas the last word, 'The meaning is in the waiting.'

Lord, forgive all the prayers I have
*   never said,*
and all the prayers that I have pretended
*   to say,*
and all the prayers that have passed me by,
and surprise me with prayer
for what remains of my day.

QUESTIONS FOR GROUPS

BIBLE READINGS: Mark 11.24-25 and Matthew 6.5-13

1. How do you rate yourself in the prayer stakes? Do you think David is too hard on himself when he says he's 'hopeless' at it?

2. David tells how the hymn *Jesu, lover of my soul* affected him as a child. Have hymns or music ever affected you in any way? Do you feel the music or words of hymns count as prayers?

3. Do the comments on track 32 of the CD ring any bells with you as far as prayer is concerned?

4. What do you make of the *Jeremy J & Christopher C* poem [track 35 and the whole poem on p. 15]? What do you think Jeremy would think of Christopher?

5. What do you hope for in prayer [tracks 37 & 38]?

6. R S Thomas' poem and the Michael Ramsey story (both on p. 16) point to the importance of perseverance and time when praying and suggest that the apparent rewards may appear quite small. Is this how you find prayer?

7. David talks about prayer 'surprising' him and 'finding' him. Does this make sense to you [track 40]?

8. David also talks of prayer as a joy rather than a duty. Does that strike a chord?

9. Do you ever end prayer more puzzled than when you began it (David calls it feeling 'addled')? David suggests this may be that prayer is drawing you 'more into the centre of the storm'. What do you make of that?

10. Have you had answers to prayer? What were they?

11. David urges us to stick at prayer, however much we feel we fail, because 'at the end of our day, prayer is all that matters'. Is it?

SESSION 4
Expecting Christ in the end

A good question

How is it all going to end? A good question for Advent, a time when we focus on the end, the last things, God's final judgement. On the subject of endings, here are three starters for ten:

1. I warmed to Cardinal Basil Hume for several reasons, not least because when he was appointed Cardinal Archbishop of Westminster in 1976 and a reporter asked him what his first priority was, he quipped: 'To set the date of my retirement'!

2. Alan Bennett's clergy wife, in his monologue *Bed amongst the Lentils*, recalls how, as a young girl, she had her later life all mapped out. By fifty she would have turned into a wonderful woman, wife either to a doctor or a vicar, inevitably multi-tasking, including being Chair of the Parish Council and leading light in the WI. She imagines herself as 'wise, witty and ultimately white-haired', maintaining her independence into her ninth decade, until, leaving the county library with an armful of improving books, she falls and breaks her hip, and dies 'peacefully, continently and without fuss,' nestling under a cosy eiderdown in her local cottage hospital. And as people leave her funeral on the sunniest of afternoons, they all say, to a man and a woman, 'Well, she was a wonderful woman!'

I'm sorry to say it doesn't often end like that. Nearly every death is either too soon or too late and it's nobody's fault. Death, like birth, brooks no management.

But can we be like Alan Bennett's vicar's wife, and dream of the end we desire, and let that end fashion us? That's got a technical term – eschatology: the last things driving our now.

3. The short-story writer Saki (HH Munro), specialises in marvellous endings. How about this: his closing words from *The Secret Sin of Septimus Brope*, a story about a very serious church music composer who makes his money anonymously writing pop ditties:

A few weeks later, in Blackpool and places where they sing, the following refrain held undisputed sway:

> *'How you bore me, Florrie*
> *With those eyes of vacant blue;*
> *You'll be very sorry, Florrie,*
> *If I marry you.*
> *Though I'm easy going, Florrie,*
> *This I swear is true,*
> *I'll throw you down a quarry, Florrie,*
> *If I marry you.'*

Or this one:

> *'If he was trying German irregular verbs on the poor elephant,' said Clovis, 'he deserved all he got.'*

We're good at beginnings and middles but tend to run out of steam by the end. I have to read a lot, and often I prioritise what I read by starting an article at the end and seeing whether it's still got punch. If it hasn't, then I move on to something that has. I guess I get the trick from God, whose first language is Hebrew and which is a back-to-front, right-to-left language, with Hebrew books ending where ours start.

But putting Hebrew aside, our faith is fired by a Gospel which starts at good endings like Golgothas, Resurrections and Ascensions. T S Eliot is so true with his line *The end is where we start from*. On a lighter note, a newspaper critic overheard this conversation between two ladies following a performance of the musical *Jesus Christ Superstar*: 'This is the second time I've watched the show – but it's so much more meaningful when you know how it ends.'!

When it comes to relationships, endings seem hard and cruel yet, when we think about it, such endings are part and parcel of every single day. Babies become toddlers, who become children, who become adults. Each day we all change, stamina comes and goes, reason comes and goes.

A former Archbishop of York, John Habgood, used to talk of all gifts being given, and being given us for just a season – schools, health, faculties, friendships, even life itself and opportunities for discipleship, given us for just a season.

The South African writer, Alan Paton, wrote a very long poem, about his son who was on the brink of adolescence and adulthood, *Meditation for a Young Boy Confirmed*. There's a particular line from the poem which has stuck with me: *'Thanks be to God for this so brief possession, so full of joy.'* That's a good bittersweet line to mark every ending.

How's it all going to end?

I come across some sad sour endings. How about these which I quote without comment:

- 'The Church in Wales doesn't value my gifts, so I am moving elsewhere.'
- 'When I was ordained it was men-only ministry. You've changed the rules without consulting me.'
- 'I'm not taking Communion from him, he's coloured.' (The lady who spat that out died the next day.)

A good parson

But the sour endings are eclipsed by a plethora of good endings. I think of Parson Woodforde who kept a diary in his Norfolk parish, Weston Longville, during the latter half of the eighteenth century – a joyous piece from beginning to end.

Without fail he entertained a half-dozen old men to Christmas dinner. I took a register of the 27 Christmases Woodforde did this, and noted a total of 22 guests because, though old and frail, many names crop up time and time again, such as Tom Carr, who, though allegedly in extremis, enjoyed 17 Christmas dinners! Then in 1793 the diary, without sentiment, records his last Christmas dinner on this earth: 'Tom Carr had his dinner sent him, being v. ill.'

By Christmas 1801 Woodforde is an old man feasting with old men, noting with sorrow, as he does on many Christmases, the failure of the Lord of the Manor and his family to mark our Lord's birth: 'None from Weston House at church today.'

Christmas 1802 sees the diary blank for the first time. On New Year's Day 1803, James Woodforde dies, having fed 150 poor folk with the Christmas dinner during his incumbency. 'Pray God, ever continue to me the power of doing good,' is his Christmas day entry 1783.

How's it all going to end?

Like any vicar I used to take out home Communions. In theory you were taking it to people in extremis. In practice you were often vying with the Ringtons Tea Man and the hairdresser! When I first began at Helmsley in 1997, I took Communion to a severely disabled old dear who looked as if she hadn't got long for this world. But she was like Tom Carr in that I ended up taking her Communion every fortnight for the next eleven years! And in a sense her eleven-year ending was a remarkable one, spanning 300 Communions.

We always used the Book of Common Prayer which has some remarkable Gospels:

eleven times she heard me tell
    of eleven prodigal sons being
    welcomed home;
eleven wounded Jews being tended by
    eleven good Samaritans;
eleven Bartimaeuses receiving their
    sight;
eleven Jairus' daughters being raised.

She was quite forthright and would interrupt the service to give her opinion on the Gospel, invariably perceptive.

It transpired during our many conversations that she had been the Forces Sweetheart, with boyfriend after boyfriend from the RAF station near York. It was her misfortune that boyfriend after boyfriend had been killed serving in Bomber Command. In the living room where we celebrated communion there was a massive picture of a Lancaster Bomber flying over the Wash coming home. All her boyfriends returning safely home: in her dreams!

How is it all going to end?

She had fallen out with her son and they hadn't spoken for twenty years, and we often talked about that. One Boxing Day, her birthday, after I had given her Christmas Communion he walked in and she welcomed him home with open arms.

She died that Easter.

How is it all going to end?

As I said, I admired Cardinal Basil Hume. In an earlier incarnation in the 1950s he had been curate of Helmsley, my previous parish, and after celebrating Mass used to have a cuppa with a lovely couple, who kept the key of the Roman Catholic Chapel. In the 1990s I ended up taking Communion to the by then very frail couple. Jack used to regale me with his tales of when he had served in the Royal Navy during World War II, including seeing his brother's ship, HMS *Hood*, torpedoed, with his brother and so many other sailors tragically losing their lives. His wife Mary was very frail and simply looked lovingly at her husband, her face radiant, as if she was hearing his tales for the first time.

When Mary died I wrote to Basil Hume to tell him, and that they often spoke of his cheering visits around their hearth. He replied by return, a two-page handwritten letter of heartfelt sympathy which I passed on to Jack, Mary's husband, who wept when he read it. Basil Hume also died that year.

How is it all going to end?

A good end

Two years back my dad, like me a priest, died. His final half-hour was amazing, with my brother and I holding him throughout. By that time Dad really did have nothing, no dignity, no possessions, all that he had was in the proverbial two carrier bags! I anointed him. I hadn't brought a stock of oil, but being a bishop, albeit a baby one, I consecrated some there and then and immediately anointed him – I can imagine St Peter at heaven's gates quipping, 'Cor, we've never had one as fresh as this before!'

Dad died of pneumonia, and for the final 24 hours breathing had been a struggle, every breath had been a groan. But in the final half-hour the groan changed key subtly and became a song. Admittedly a song on just one note, but there again, vicars are used to singing songs on one note:

O Lord, open thou our lips …

I suddenly realised that this was Dad's evensong, his last evensong sung at the eve of his life.

But more than the song there was the look, which was no less than a look of rapture, in stark contrast to the pain that had dogged his final weeks. It was what I term a *tetelestai* moment. In John's Gospel, as he breathes his last Jesus says *'tetelestai'* – *'it is accomplished'*. Except that in the original Greek *telos* means so much more than that: the whole purpose and point and goal and end all come together.

All of a sudden Dad's life seemed to come terrifically together. It was not pointless. Heaven was his goal and there his goal lay open before him. No more pain, no more tears, no more missing his mum Emily, our mum and his wife Eileen, no more church councils – Dad always dreaded them. All of a sudden what Rowan Williams termed 'the sheer terror of existence' fell away and Dad realised the point of his existence: God had made Dad for himself and his whole body breathed a sigh of relief as it found its rest in him.

How is it all going to end?

At the Port Talbot Passion Play, in the final scene Jesus (played by Michael Sheen) was crucified, the ultimate end. But then he came back and his final words were, 'Now it begins!'

The undoubted star of Charles Dickens's *A Christmas Carol* is Tiny Tim, consumptive, crippled, clearly nearing the end, described by Dickens as 'the last of all', a studied ambiguity. Yet rather than dwelling on all his many setbacks, Tiny Tim is an icon of cheerfulness despite utter adversity, 'God bless us every one!' his rallying call.

God bless all of you who dare to pick yourselves up after tragedy and failure, who dare to expect resurrection when faced by crucifixion, who dare to expect the beginning when faced by an end, who dare to expect Christ in the end.

The Corrymeela Community in Ireland was a tremendous force for reconciliation in the midst of the Troubles. A group from one of the most troubled parts of Belfast was staying there one Easter weekend and pinned this very Irish prayer on the intercessions board on Holy Saturday:

If it wasn't for tomorrow,
yesterday would be unbearable.

I suppose our Advent prayer is that God will bless all our endings with his beginnings. God has given us his word on that in Jesus, his final Word, who ends Matthew's Gospel with the ultimate beginning: *'Remember I am with you always, until the end of the age.'*

We were talking, at a recent Bishops' meeting, about Jesus' valediction, *Go in peace.* In the Gospels this is often associated with healing and forgiveness, where Jesus marks an end to illness, sin and even death with new life with all its opportunities, in all its fullness. The New Testament Greek actually reads, *Go into peace.* Which is rather lovely. Go into Christ's peace, both at your start and your end and all stops in between.

QUESTIONS FOR GROUPS

BIBLE READING: John 6.35-40

1. Many Christian communities (especially the Orthodox) consider that preparing for death and what lies beyond should be taught from childhood. Is this unduly gloomy?

2. What would you like to read in your own obituary? [Track 44.]

3. Do any of the experiences of loved ones dying [track 45] correspond with your experiences?

4. David defines eschatology as *'the last things driving our now'*. How realistic is it to decide how we want things to end and to live our lives in tune with our end in mind?

5. T S Eliot's line *'The end is where we start from'* is very famous, but what does it mean? And is it true?

6. John Habgood said that all gifts are given us for just a season. This seems to link in with the idea in the line from Alan Paton's poem (p.21) – *Thanks be to God for this so brief possession, so full of joy.* Does this make sense to you, and do you find it helpful?

7. Parson Woodforde would have been good company by the sound of things! Many people have found generous hospitality to be a great blessing and a natural way to discover the nature of Christ. Have you experienced this? If so, please tell the story. And how can the Church do more of it, more effectively?

8. Is there a heaven [tracks 49 & 50]?

9. David's description of his father's death is very moving. Do you have recollections of 'good deaths' (or otherwise) that you would be prepared to share with the group?

10. Should we talk more about death and dying [track 53]?

11. On p. 23 in one short paragraph the word 'dare' is used four times. If you think about it, it may seem a rather strange word to use about faith. It suggests that there is risk in expecting such things. Is there a risk in expectation, and what might it be?

12. What is the difference between *going in peace* and *going into peace*?

13. As this course comes to an end, you might want to plan ahead as a discussion group, a church or a group of churches.

You may like to end with this passage: Romans 8.31-39.

" … the excellent series of York Courses
designed for groups and individuals. " *Church Times* review

YORK COURSES

have an extensive list of ecumenical courses, suitable for all seasons – including Lent and Advent. All are ideal for discussion groups, and individual reflection. The majority of our courses have 5 sessions, but there are 4- and 6-session courses too, and the range is growing every year. There's something for everyone! All of the following have a course booklet with questions, plus an accompanying CD and transcript.

5-SESSION COURSE
IDEAL FOR LENT – or any time of year

BUILD ON THE ROCK
Faith, doubt – and Jesus

starts by looking at faith and doubt. Is it wrong – or is it normal and healthy – for a Christian to have doubts? Is there any evidence for a God who loves us? We hear from many witnesses. At the heart of a Christian answer stands Jesus himself. We consider his 'strange and beautiful story' and reflect upon his teaching, his death, his resurrection and his continuing significance.

With Bishop Richard Chartres, Dr Paula Gooder, Revd Joel Edwards and Revd David Gamble.

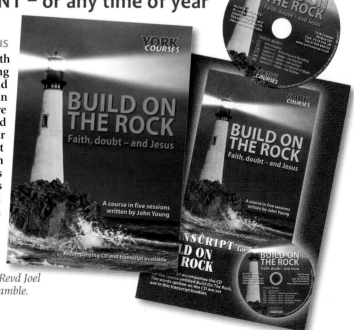

5-SESSION COURSES

GLIMPSES OF GOD
Hope for today's world
Course booklet written by Canon David Winter
We live in turbulent times. This course draws on the Bible, showing where we can find strength and encouragement as we live through the 21st century.
With Rt Hon Shirley Williams, Bishop Stephen Cottrell, Revd Professor David Wilkinson and Revd Lucy Winkett.

HANDING ON THE TORCH
Sacred words for a secular world
Worldwide Christianity continues to grow at an immense pace. At the same time in the West it struggles to grow and – perhaps – even to survive. But what might this mean for individual Christians, churches and Western culture, in a world where alternative beliefs are increasingly on offer?
With Archbishop Sentamu, Clifford Longley, Rachel Lampard and Bishop Graham Cray.

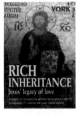

RICH INHERITANCE
Jesus' legacy of love
Course booklet written by Bishop Stephen Cottrell
Jesus left no written instructions. By most worldly estimates his ministry was a failure. Nevertheless, Jesus' message of reconciliation with God lives on. With this good news his disciples changed the world. What else did Jesus leave behind – what is his 'legacy of love'?
With Archbishop Vincent Nichols, Paula Gooder, Jim Wallis and Inderjit Bhogal.

WHEN I SURVEY...
Christ's cross and ours
Course booklet written by Revd Dr John Pridmore
The death of Christ is a dominant and dramatic theme in the New Testament. The death of Jesus is not the end of a track – it's the gateway into life.
With General Sir Richard Dannatt, John Bell, Christina Baxter and Colin Morris.

These three...
FAITH, HOPE & LOVE

Based on the three great qualities celebrated in 1 Corinthians 13. This famous passage begins and ends in majestic prose. But the middle paragraph is practical and demanding. St Paul's thirteen verses take us to the heart of what it means to be a Christian.
With Bp Tom Wright, Anne Atkins, the Abbot of Worth and Professor Frances Young.

THE LORD'S PRAYER
praying it, meaning it, living it
In the Lord's Prayer Jesus gives us a pattern for living as his disciples. It also raises vital questions for today's world in which 'daily bread' is uncertain for billions and a refusal to 'forgive those who trespass against us' escalates violence.

With Canon Margaret Sentamu, Bishop Kenneth Stevenson, Dr David Wilkinson and Dr Elaine Storkey.

CAN WE BUILD A BETTER WORLD?
We live in a divided world and with a burning question. As modern Christians can we – together with others of good will – build a better world? Important material for important issues.
With Archbishop John Sentamu, Wendy Craig, Leslie Griffiths and five Poor Clares from BBC TV's 'The Convent'.

WHERE IS GOD...?
To find honest answers to these big questions we need to undertake some serious and open thinking. Where better to do this than with trusted friends in a study group around this course?
With Archbishop Rowan Williams, Patricia Routledge CBE, Joel Edwards and Dr Pauline Webb.

BETTER TOGETHER?
Course booklet written by Revd David Gamble

All about relationships – in the church and within family and society. *Better Together?* looks at how the Christian perspective may differ from that of society at large.

With the Abbot of Ampleforth, John Bell, Nicky Gumbel and Jane Williams.

TOUGH TALK
Hard Sayings of Jesus

Looks at many of the hard sayings of Jesus in the Bible and faces them squarely. His uncomfortable words need to be faced if we are to allow the full impact of the gospel on our lives.

With Bishop Tom Wright, Steve Chalke, Fr Gerard Hughes SJ and Professor Frances Young.

NEW WORLD, OLD FAITH

How does Christian faith continue to shed light on a range of issues in our changing world, including change itself? This course helps us make sense of our faith in God in today's world.

With Archbishop Rowan Williams, David Coffey, Joel Edwards, Revd Dr John Polkinghorne KBE FRS and Dr Pauline Webb.

IN THE WILDERNESS

Like Jesus, we all have wilderness experiences. What are we to make of these challenges? *In the Wilderness* explores these issues for our world, for the church, and at a personal level.

With Cardinal Cormac Murphy-O'Connor, Archbishop David Hope, Revd Dr Rob Frost, Roy Jenkins and Dr Elaine Storkey.

FAITH IN THE FIRE

When things are going well our faith may remain untroubled, but what if doubt or disaster strike? Those who struggle with faith will find they are not alone.

With Archbishop David Hope, Rabbi Lionel Blue, Steve Chalke, Revd Dr Leslie Griffiths and Ann Widdecombe MP and Lord George Carey.

JESUS REDISCOVERED

Re-discovering who Jesus was, what he taught, and what that means for his followers today. Some believers share what Jesus means to them.

With Paul Boateng MP, Dr Lavinia Byrne, Joel Edwards, Bishop Tom Wright and Archbishop David Hope.

6-SESSION COURSES

LIVE YOUR FAITH
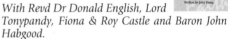

Christianity isn't just about what we believe: it's about how we live. A course suitable for everyone; particularly good for enquirers and those in the early stages of their faith.

With Revd Dr Donald English, Lord Tonypandy, Fiona & Roy Castle and Baron John Habgood.

GREAT EVENTS, DEEP MEANINGS

Explains clearly what the feasts and fasts are about and challenges us to respond spiritually and practically. There are even a couple of quizzes to get stuck into!

With Revd Dr John Polkinghorne KBE FRS, Gordon Wilson, Bishop David Konstant, Fiona Castle, Dame Cicely Saunders, Archbishop David Hope.

❝The York Courses are a good brand. They help remind church members of their faith, serve useful sharing on Christian basics and engage with big issues.❞
Revd John Twisleton

YORK COURSES

also have **CD Conversations** featuring leading Christian thinkers, **books** and **booklets**. A selection of these is shown below to whet your appetite. Please visit www.yorkcourses.co.uk where detailed information on the full range is available, and you can listen to sound bites from the CDs, and view sample pages from our course booklets and transcripts, as well as order online.

CD CONVERSATIONS

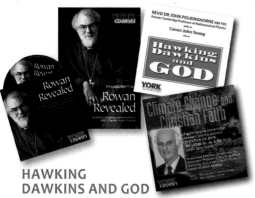

HAWKING DAWKINS AND GOD

Revd Dr John Polkinghorne KBE FRS, an Anglican Priest and Fellow of the Royal Society, discusses his Christian faith in the light of the New Atheism and explains why he believes in God.

ROWAN REVEALED

The 104th Archbishop of Canterbury talks about his life and faith, prayer, the press, politics, the future of the Church ...

CLIMATE CHANGE AND CHRISTIAN FAITH

Nobel Prize winner Sir John Houghton CBE, FRS, a world expert on global warming, talks about why he believes in Climate Change and in Jesus Christ.

ALSO AVAILABLE AS MULTIPACKS.

PAPERBACKS BY JOHN YOUNG

LORD... HELP MY UNBELIEF

"John Young is an outstanding communicator of the Christian message"
(Canon David Winter)

CHRISTIANITY – AN INTRODUCTION

"An exciting, engaging and intellectually serious book" *(Archbishop Rowan Williams)*

CHRISTIANITY MADE SIMPLE

A short and to-the-point guide to Christianity, set out in just 96 pages.

Please contact our office for a current copy of our full list of courses and publications, including prices.

T: **01904 466516** / E: **courses@yorkcourses.co.uk**

Or download a copy from **www.yorkcourses.co.uk**